Preserving Biodiversity

*The role of economics in
international environmental
policy-making*

Brian Meadows

Revive Publications

A catalogue record for this book is available from the British Library

ISBN: 978-1-907962-09-7

Published by Revive Publications

Reading, England

For Matt

Contents

5

Preface

Preserving biodiversity is one of the main objectives on the international environmental agenda. There are many factors which need to be considered if this objective is to be achieved.

In this book I explore the role that economics plays in international environmental policy-making; this is because economics is the key factor that affects the amount of biodiversity that exists on the Earth.

Introduction

The issue of biodiversity will be used to evaluate the extent to which economic considerations determine the outcome of international environmental policy-making. A brief outline of the biodiversity issue is to be found in *Chapter One*. Then, in *Chapter Two*, the view that economic considerations prevail in international environmental policy-making is outlined. The counter-arguments that economic considerations do no inevitably prevail are then outlined in *Chapter Three*. In *Chapter Four* several biodiversity examples are considered to investigate whether policy-making can result in both economic and environmental objectives being achieved. In *Chapter Five* an evaluation is made concerning the extent to which economic considerations prevail in international environmental policy-making.

Chapter 1

Biodiversity as an Environmental Problem

Biodiversity is a term that describes the whole array of differing life-forms that exist on the planet. There are three different aspects to biodiversity – species diversity, ecosystem diversity and genetic diversity. In recent times through a combination of high consumption levels, high population levels, harmful technologies and a widespread individualis-tic/nature-detached social construction, humans have inflicted massive damage to biodiversity.

Habitat destruction, transformation and segmentation have caused a massive reduction in species diversity and genetic diversity. The speed of the anthropogenic changes has meant that organisms have been unable to adapt and have thus become extinct. The contemporary extinction rate has been estimated to be between 10,000 and 20,000 species per annum (Barnes, 1996, p. 221). This loss of biodiversity is a major environmental problem.

Chapter 2

The Prevalence of Economic Considerations in International Environmental Policy-Making

Whilst economic considerations are fundamental causal factors behind the biodiversity loss problem it can also be argued that economic considerations prevail in international environmental policy-making. In order to understand the motivations of policy-makers it is necessary to understand the economic basis of the international system. Capitalism is driven by the economic processes of immanent development which inevitably lead to globalization and escalating global trade. In this scenario firms are impelled to both over-exploit individual species in a particular location – as the example of the export of frogs' legs from Bangladesh makes clear – and to displace local sustainable management systems of biodiversity with unsustainable and biodiversity degrading methods that are necessary for international competitiveness (Barnes, 1996, pp. 226-228).

Furthermore, the competitiveness inherent in the system compels sovereign states to seek to ensure the competitive position of their firms so that their GNP can be maximised. Thus in international environmental policy-making despite the objective being the common good individual nations seek to maximise their own economic benefits at the expense of others. If a country's economy is likely to be hurt by a policy it is likely that they will either refuse to participate in the policy, or only participate if economy-friendly amendments are made. The potential for adverse economic impacts from environmental policymaking also exacerbates the 'free rider' problem whereby countries are reluctant to take the initiative in policy-making (Beukering and Vellinga, 1996, p. 214). Thus the international capitalist system both causes significant losses of biodiversity and prevents effective solutions to the problem at an international level due to the prominence of economic considerations.

In any policy-making process the issue of which agents are the most powerful is of central importance as these agents are usually able to achieve their objectives. In international environmental policy-making the countries of the 'developed' world are the most powerful due to their economic wealth. Thus international policies are inevitably agreeable to their continued economic success, and are often at the expense of both the environment and the 'developing' countries. This can be illustrated through two examples of policy-making where issues of biodiversity are of great importance - biotechnology and global warming.

The issue of biotechnology became an international environmental policy-making issue in Nassau in 1994 at the first Conference of Parties to the Convention on Biological Diversity. There are major uncertainties concerning the effects that genetically engineered crops may have on natural biodiversity; gene silencing, 'positional effects' and 'pleiotropy' are just some of the inherent uncertainties involved (WWF International, 1995, pp. 12-14). The concept of trans-science is therefore applicable and the precautionary principle should be adhered to so that natural biodiversity can be protected. Despite this the technology has been pushed through by the 'developed' countries as their firms are at the forefront of the technology, and thus it enables them to further enhance their economic domination over the 'developing' countries. The case of US company

Calgene producing high-lauric oilseed rape so that imports from developing countries can be reduced is one example (WWF International, 1995, pp. 12-14). According to the OECD: "there is strong evidence that developing countries, notably those heavily involved in agriculture, will bear the brunt of trade impacts for a long time to come" (WWF International, 1995, pp. 12-14).

The issue of global warming is another very good example of how the economic needs of the most powerful countries are prioritised over biodiversity, and the interests of the developing countries, in international environmental policy-making. There is a strong scientific consensus in the IPCC about both the occurrence of anthropogenic climate alteration and the devastating effects this will entail for biodiversity. Yet two of the countries with the most to lose economically from implementing international limitation policies – the US and Russia – have decided to prioritise their economic position in the world order over the right of all life-forms to enjoy a relatively stable long-term climate. They have used the inherent uncertainties in the climate system as an excuse for not taking real action on climate change, but the real reason is concern for future economic growth. The relatively powerless developing countries are, as with the biotechnology case, the main losers; they are particularly vulnerable to sea-level rises and meteorological changes, and they lack funds for adaptation policies.

The developing countries, as the relatively powerless agents in international environmental policy-making, thus often bear the environmental consequences of economic considerations in the developed countries. However, it needs to be stressed that economic considerations in international environmental policy-making are even more important for the developing countries than for the developed. This is due to the overriding requirement for development and poverty alleviation in developing countries. Thus in the FCCC the developing countries have utilised the principle of common but differentiated responsibilities to seek to expand their carbon dioxide emissions for economic purposes, whilst also seeking financial and technological transfers from the developed countries. Furthermore, countries like Bangladesh have been more than willing to trade their biodiversity for international currency. The mass export of frogs from Bangladesh exemplifies the way in which developing countries prioritise economic considerations over their biodiversity (Barnes, 1996, p. 228).

There are strong underlying motivations for all states involved in environmental policy-making to pursue their own economic agenda.

Chapter 3

Non-Economic Considerations in International Environmental Policy-Making

We have seen that underlying economic motivations, in conjunction with rising affluence in the North and an escalating population in the South, have caused ecological damage. This ecological damage has become so large, so pervasive, that it has resulted in the creation of an opposing environmental awareness paradigm. This paradigm, as the antithesis of the economic exploitation paradigm, involves an appreciation of the intrinsic value of biodiversity and is grounded in ethics and a spiritual appreciation of the aesthetic value of nature. The emergence of this paradigm means that in international environmental policy-making there is a countervailing power base which can result in economic considerations not always prevailing due to concern for biodiversity itself and for future generations of humans.

This countervailing power base is effectively exercised through environmental NGOs, who in an era of globalised media and communications, are increasingly able to exert power on governments to prioritise environmental objectives. These NGOs are able to generate even greater public awareness of anthropogenic impacts through campaigns such as the WWFs 'Adopt a Tiger' campaign. The growing awareness of the intrinsic, spiritual, aesthetic and anthropocentric values of biodiversity has led to specific international and global measures which have biodiversity protection as their overriding objective. One example is the partnership between the WWF and the World Bank to increase the percentage of forests in protected areas to ten per cent.

At a regional level the EU has formulated many policies that are directly aimed at biodiversity protection. The first piece of EU legislation targeted specifically at biodiversity was The Birds Directive of 1979. The legislation covered habitat availability, control of hunting and killing of wild birds and safeguarding eggs in nests. The CITES Regulation seeks to protect endangered biodiversity through ensuring that the Convention on International Trade in Endangered Species is enforced in the EU. Species of flora and fauna that are considered as being of Union-wide interest are protected under the 1992 Habitats Directive, which also seeks to establish a network of protected habitats across Europe. The Environmental Impact Assessment Directive is important as it requires developers of major projects to investigate the whole range of environmental impacts of their proposed project. If the biodiversity and ecosystem impacts are found to be too great then the potential economic benefits of the project will be foregone (Barnes, 1996, pp. 237-238).

At a global level the Convention on Biological Diversity was formulated at the Rio Earth Summit in 1992. The convention is an attempt to achieve an integrated global approach to biodiversity management. It requires signatory states to formulate their own strategies to conserve biodiversity, with significant funds available through the Global Environmental Facility to help states achieve their strategies.

There are thus political pressures emanating from individual social constructions of acceptable and sustainable human behaviour that when aggregated, and particularly when channelled through NGOs and/or the EU, result in environmental considerations prevailing in national, regional and global policies. The role of biodiversity in maintaining global security through providing endowments to people in developing countries, coined by Mittermeier and Bowles as 'ecosecurity' (Barnes, 1996, p. 232) is another reason why political concerns will be prioritised over economic factors in international environmental policy-making. However, there is a big difference between political factors prevailing in the policy process and there being the political will to expend the resources that may be necessary to implement the policy. In this way despite being subjugated in the policy process economic considerations may still prevail. This problem is clear in the case of the trade in the diminishing tiger population despite the CITES legislation (TRAFFIC International, 1994, pp. 47-49). Economic considerations were subjugated in the policy-forming process, yet, in reality, economic considerations are still causing the trade in tigers to continue.

Chapter 4

The Joint Achievement of Economic and Environmental Objectives

We have seen that there is a tendency for economic considerations to ultimately prevail, even if environmental considerations prevail in international environmental policy-making. Because of this attempts have been made to integrate the two sets of considerations.

In the long-term economic objectives and environmental objectives are clearly concordant. This appreciation has been utilised to attempt to achieve both sets of objectives in the short-term, as is encapsulated by the notion of sustainable development. A good example is the utilisation of honey and caterpillars by local people in Kasungu National Park (Barnes, 1996, p. 240). A more widely applicable fusion of the objectives may be achieved by a proper valuation of the economic benefits of biodiversity. Bennet and Reynolds (Barnes, 1996, p. 239) concluded that if selected high biodiversity mangroves in Sarawak were valued for their economic benefits of timber production, tourism potential, flood protection, fisheries and employment that the mangroves would be protected on economic criteria. Therefore, proper valuation leads to both environmental and economic objectives being fulfilled.

However, in other attempts at integration the economic considerations can be argued to be dominant. For example, the 'no regrets' limitation policies utilized in climate change policy-making restrict action on environmental objectives to the level at which economic objectives are not harmed. So, despite the attempts in international fisheries policy-making to achieve a sustainable yield over time, via the bionomic fisheries model, the underlying economic incentives result in unsustainable fishing levels (Anand, 2003, pp. 108-9).

Debt-for-nature swaps are a theoretically appealing way of achieving both the biodiversity objectives of the North and the economic objectives of the South. As the North got rich by depleting biodiversity, transferring part of this wealth to the South to conserve a great part of the remaining biodiversity seems to be a logical policy. Criticisms can be made of such a scheme but the objections do not appear to be of overwhelming significance.

Chapter 5

Evaluation

The range of biodiversity issues that have been considered can be used to evaluate the extent to which economic considerations prevail in international environmental policy-making. In a highly competitive international capitalist system power relations have been highly significant in shaping policy outcomes. Power is evident in both the capacity of firms to shape national and international policy, and the capacity of the North to shape global policy. The power of firms and the need for governments to raise living standards has led to the prioritization of economic objectives across the world in many areas of environmental policy-making. Furthermore, the power of the North has often resulted in positive economic outcomes for the North allied to negative economic and environmental outcomes for the South. The issues of biotechnology, the mass export of frogs from Bangladesh and global warming have been used to illustrate these points. These power relations can seem to make the prevalence of economic considerations inevitable.

However, the emergence of the environmental awareness paradigm has resulted in a countervailing power base in the political process due to concern for biodiversity and future generations of humans.

This paradigm has led to a range of international environmental policies that are solely concerned with environmental criteria. Several such policies have been outlined both at EU level and globally. This paradigm has also reduced the likelihood of economic considerations prevailing in all areas of environmental policy-making. The Environmental Impact Assessment Directive is a prime example of the shift away from economic prevalence inevitability. Economic objectives will also be subjugated to the political need for biodiversity as 'ecosecurity'.

When policies are in the implementation stage, and when attempts are made to integrate economic and environmental objectives, the ascendancy of economic considerations is often revealed. The issues of declining tiger populations and overfishing are evidence of this. However, as the case of the proper valuation of the economic benefits of biodiversity in Sarawak makes clear, environmental protection can make economic sense. In this case economic considerations prevailing is good for the environment. The implementation of debt-for-nature swaps also involves the economic considerations of the South prevailing in order to meet the environmental objectives of the North. The prevalence of economic considerations is therefore not inevitably bad for the environment.

Therefore economic considerations do not inevitably prevail in international environmental policy-making; there are various political considerations that may take precedence. There are also many policies which have the sole objective of environmental protection. Furthermore, economic valuation can also lead to environmental protection despite economic considerations prevailing. However, due to the nature of the international capitalist system, economic considerations do generally prevail, and this is typically at the expense of environmental considerations.

Bibliography

Anand, P. (2003) 'Economic analysis and environmental responses' in Blowers, A. and Hinchcliffe, S. (eds) *Environmental Responses*, Chichester, John Wiley & Sons/The Open University.

Barnes, N. (1996) 'Conflicts over biodiversity' in Sloep, P. and Blowers, A. (eds) *Environmental Policy in an International Context: Conflicts*, London, Arnold.

Beukering, P. and Vellinga, P. (1996) 'Climate change: From science to global policies' in Sloep, P. and Blowers, A. (eds) *Environmental Policy in an International Context: Conflicts*, London, Arnold.

TRAFFIC International (1994) 'Killed for a Cure: A Review of the Worldwide Trade in Tiger Bone', Cambridge, TRAFFIC International.

WWF International (1995) 'Genetic engineering: examples of ecological effects and inherent uncertainties', Gland, Switzerland, WWF International.

Other books by the author:

Sustainable Development & GM Food: An analysis of the relationship between the genetic modification of crops and the varieties of sustainable development (2011)

www.ingramcontent.com/pod-product-compliance
Lightning Source LLC
Chambersburg PA
CBHW060701280326
41933CB00012B/2261